WHO AM I?

What is my Soul?

Birth and Death

The Bridge

Fresh Mornings of life

Good Company ISBN 0-9547939-0-0

A Lasting Freedom

The Man Who Wanted To Meet God ISBN 0-517-88520-4

The Orange Book ISBN 0-9547939-3-5

Prayer

Voyage of Discovery ISBN 0-9547939-4-3

WHO AM I?

What is my Soul?

THE STUDY SOCIETY

ISBN 0-9547939-2-7

A catalogue record for this book is available
from the British Library

Published in 2005 by The Society for the
Study of Normal Psychology,
Colet House, 151 Talgarth Road, London W.14 9DA
Telephone 0208 748 9338, Fax: 0208 563 0551,
Email: colethouse@clara.net
Website: http://www.studysociety.net

The Study Society has groups around the UK,
and can also be contacted through addresses in Australia,
Mexico, New York and New Zealand

Printed in Great Britain by
Creative Print and Design (Wales), Ebbw Vale

Introduction

We are now living in a world where the interdependence of everyone and everything is becoming more and more apparent. While not a single man or woman is visible from the moon, we know all too well man's physical capacity to destroy the very fabric of this planet. Modern means of communication keep us aware of disasters as they occur. We know that what we do on one side of the world may affect the climate and livelihood of people on the other side. Global warming, the dangers inherent in the destruction of rain forests, and our need for conservation and recycling are widely accepted.

This globalisation has led to a fear of loss of identity, and individual societies, cultures, races and faiths fight to keep their independence, leading to increased confrontation and violence. Just as the variety of forms of life in the natural world appears to be a necessity for the survival of the whole, so it may be with all the varieties of the human race, and we need to realise that it is we ourselves, and not the Almighty, who are responsible for the violence in the world.

What could bring a better understanding among races and heal all the bitterness and conflict? Perhaps seeing what we have in common? That is, surely, the way we are made? Although we may have different skin colour and exterior characteristics, the one thing we do have in common is the basic structure as a human being? There is one even more basic thing we have in common and that is the source of our life force and energy.

What receives this life force and energy? Perhaps this is where that much misunderstood concept "Soul" comes in? This word has been used in so many ways and acquired so many associations that it has currently lost its relevance. Nevertheless, it can still have a deep and very simple meaning. There is knowledge which is universal and at the root of all cultures; it is not new and is present in all traditions but the practical application in simple terms has got buried in religious and philosophical language that is incomprehensible to the ordinary person; it does not relate to every day life and so is not understood and made use of.

If we could look at the structure and purpose of each and every human being on this planet – each 'made in the image of God or the Absolute' and if we could explain in the simplest terms that each and every person can fulfil his potential by 'being him/herself' and that this is the true meaning of individual freedom in a totally interdependent world, we could contribute to a tremendous change.

A better understanding of what the situation is could lead to a totally different attitude to oneself, to others, to the causes of 'evil'; to each and every person's responsibility to himself and the world around, to a great 'healing' process which could catch on and become global.

Bede Griffiths* describes this in an article he wrote "How I Pray":

('In the beginning was the Word...' John 1) I consider that this Word "enlightens everyone coming into the world", and though they may not recognise it, it is present to every human being in the depths of their soul. Beyond word and thought, beyond all signs and symbols, this Word is being secretly spoken in every heart in every place and at every time. People may be utterly ignorant of it, or may choose to ignore it, but whenever or wherever anyone responds to truth or love or kindness, to the demand for justice, concern for others, care of those in need, they are responding to the voice of the Word. So also when anyone seeks truth or beauty in science, philosophy, poetry or art, they are responding to the inspiration of the Word.

Many people are crying out for help in understanding how a so -called loving god or creator can allow all the violence manifesting in the world today. They are full of doubts and are at a loss to see where the answer lies and how they can help.

In one of the most ancient philosophies and scriptures in the world probably lies the answer, but like the truths present in all the great traditions, it is not understood practically and in terms understandable by the ordinary person. A profound and practical answer arose as a result of the meeting of a remarkable English doctor** and a man of great wisdom, the then Shankacharya of Northern India, Shantanand Saraswati.*** The latter did not preach or teach the doctor in the usual sense of the word – he simply responded to questions put by the doctor and those who visited him on the doctor's behalf. I had the great privilege of attending most of the audiences and typing up the dialogue, and of making the visits on behalf of the Doctor when he was no longer able to go.

A very large part of the questions and answers concerned the way our Minds are made under the Sanskrit term 'Antahkaran' which translates as 'inner vehicle' or, as more than once translated by the Shankaracharya himself – 'SOUL'! This has been a revelation – one talks of "poor soul", "miserable soul", "old soul" etc. but does not stop to ask oneself what the word 'soul' really means – the use in religious terminology does not seem to relate to everyday life and for me was something I would think about in relation to the end of my life, not something which related to the way I lived each and every day and would help me to understand the apparent contradictions and confusion which arose when I tried to find answers to my deepest questions. So, when I began to realise that these wonderful answers were practical and were the first time SOUL became truly topical, I felt we should make use of the permission and encouragement Shantanand Saraswati gave us to share this with others.

Shantanand Saraswati's answers open the way for anyone, of whatever race or faith, to understand the source of all the violence and manmade disasters in the world and the way towards healing and unity. They concern the way we are made and the use or misuse of our capacities.

When one has realised the basic unity of humanity I find it gives me confidence to "be" myself and gives me a new valuation and appreciation of the tradition in which I grew up – that is as a Christian. But the real change has been to find that one can be rooted in one's own faith and share so much with others of other faiths who share the same experience of unity. I have had the privilege of sharing with Muslims and Buddhists and the wonderful answers which form the basis of this booklet were from Shantanand Saraswati, late Shankaracharya of North India who, therefore, would be considered to be a Hindu.

I found the following quotation on the Internet but no source, but feel the author would approve of it being used in this context:

"From the point of view of Advaita (non-dualism) or monism, the real Self is the Divine Reality, itself non-different from the Godhead. The purpose of spiritual life is to purify, unify and transform the instrument, that is the mind, so that the Self can be realized as it is in itself – pure and infinite."

MAUREEN ALLAN

Quotations from Audiences with His Holiness Shantanand Saraswati

Note: The first time the Sanskrit term for 'Soul' (Antahkaran) was used it was unfamiliar. In the following quotations every time the Sanskrit word was used it has been translated as *Soul* and put in italics. All the quotations given below were answers to questions put to Shantanand Saraswati during audiences granted from 1962 to 1993. Capital letters are used for certain terms to give them emphasis and to give them a special meaning – this was done in the original record and have been retained in this version. The answers are potent and very rich in content and it may be that the best way to benefit from them is to just take one or two at a time and go over them more than once.

The body can never have communion with the divine; it is only through the *Soul* that a man will have experience of communion

Each one of us lives in three kinds of bodies – physical, subtle or psychological, and causal. The inner organ of mind belongs to the causal body. Functionally the inner organ of mind consists of four parts: -

the discriminating part or intellect,
the moving mind,
the sense of 'I'
and the memory;

but this inner organ of mind is one and the

same thing which, on being activated by the supreme power, called pure or absolute consciousness, assumes any one of the four functions and thereby acquires the corresponding name:

The moving mind is that which thinks ' I should be rich or poor, learned or ignorant etc.' It acts like an office secretary whose job is merely to put up various papers or files before the manager and his duty ends with this. The rest is not his concern and belongs to the realm of other departments of the inner organ of mind.

Memory is that which thinks over what the moving mind presents; what would be favourable and what would be unfavourable.

Intellect or discrimination is that which takes decisions. These decisions govern actions.

'I' thought is of two kinds – pure and impure. The impure is that which makes us believe ' I am this physical body', 'I am great or small', 'black or white, rich or poor, learned or ignorant etc.' Pure 'I' thought is that which identifies itself with the Self or the Universal Self. Everything is only that and yet it is neither this nor that. For example, the banana is a fruit, but we can call neither the skin, pulp, tree, stem nor leaves a banana and yet a thing called banana is there. Similarly 'I' am neither the hand, feet, head nor even the whole body which is made of all these. Hence 'I' which is separate from all these is pure 'I'.

The Universal Self is in each and everything and yet is neither the whole world or anything it is made up of. But it is all truth, all power, all joy – this is as far as words can go.

The Self is a part of Universal Self, possessing all the attributes of the Universal Self, just as water in a drop is a part of the ocean and is endowed with all the properties of the ocean water.

In the world today there are a multitude of ideas prevailing and everybody stands up to declare his principles and wants to lead everybody else according to his own principles, and others are also trying to state their own! In this situation there is, of course, need for a man who is not involved in any ideological victory who might fill the role.

There were ten men crossing a fast river, and when they reached the other side they started counting themselves to make sure that all had reached the other side safely. Each one counted but found only nine, because he did not count himself; and they became very worried. Just at that time a holy man passed by and, looking at their miserable faces, asked what was wrong? They told him and demonstrated how there were only nine of them, though they had started as ten. He made them stand in line and with his stick he hit the first man once and separated him from the line. He hit the second one twice, and so on till the last one. He hit him ten times and declared he was the tenth one. They were very happy and went on their way.

The same situation today prevails in the world – these ten men, or ten ideologies mean the numerous ideologies which are prevailing – each counting all the others without looking at themselves, so they all like to keep on fighting. Unless somebody else comes out and hits each of them hard to bring them to their senses, this situation will go on.

Q. The first time we heard this story the Shankaracharya went on to tell us "Before we could know who we are, we have to learn to come out of what we are not." We have begun to see some of the things we are <u>not</u>, but how can we begin to see what we are?

S. Whenever one has lost something in the physical sense one has to get some light to look for it and find it. There are many different types of light of which one can make use – a small lamp, a lantern, electric light, moonlight and sunlight. One of these would do according to the type of thing which one is looking for. They are sufficient for the physical world.

In the subtle world of mind, memory and discrimination, if one has lost anything there one has to get the light of Knowledge, the light of the subtle world and with that light one can find what one has lost. As far as the Self is concerned, the Self is always experienced by everyone whether one is lost in the physical darkness, or within the subtle darkness of ignorance. In each case the Self is always experienced and present – one does not need any other agency to find out the Self and experience the Self, and no -one can deny the existence of the Self, because there is no other means of denying it except the Self! The situation is that the Self is always available and whatever is available and experienced does not need any extra light. The light we need is only on the physical and subtle levels. For that we can take the physical light or the subtle light of Knowledge from the scriptures, from a Realized Man, or teachers. Even with knowledge, if the knowledge is not complete we still cannot transcend the subtle world and in that way transcend to the reality beyond this subtle world, so the proper experience of the Self is not constant and continuous. The Self is eternal and the Self is the Light of Lights. The Self is Consciousness, and the Self is happiness. It is eternal and it is Truth, and all these things are never lost because they are ever present everywhere. One has simply to dispel the physical darkness or the subtle darkness which is prevailing, because the Self is always with each of us. Let the Self prevail, there is no need to search for it.

Q. The Shankaracharya has given us to much wonderful knowledge, and we would like to make best use of this. From what he has seen of us by our questions, could he say what might be the best line of study for us to continue?

S. Before studying anything else one has to study the Self. One has to study one's physical body, and one's subtle body and look within to the causal body. There is nothing else to study so no line of study is prescribed. Whatever may be useful according to the place and time, and the type of literature which pleases you or seems to satisfy you, you can get help from them. It can come from any source, it makes no difference. <u>The emphasis is the Self and the non -self.</u> One has to study the Self so as to separate the non-self – one has to experience happiness so as to leave behind misery and unhappiness. One has to find Truth to leave behind untruth. One has to find what is useful to the True Self and make use of it and discard what is not useful to the True Self. These are the ways one can study

Referring to the True Self and its opposite – if one took Ganges water in a bottle it would be clear and pure. If one added a drop of red colour then the whole water would be red. If one added a drop of green it would become brown, and if one went on adding more and more colours, after a time one would find it looked brownish -grey, and one would not be able to recognise the pure clear Ganges water. One could leave this water and the dust might subside, but the colour would not disappear. One has to add some sort of alum to decolourize or clarify the whole thing and only then would one be able to see pure clean Ganges water. The True Self is very much like Ganges water which is pure and clean, but it is surrounded by the *Soul* with its memory, discrimination, moving mind and senses of knowledge, action, the elements, and every-thing one has taken from society. One has to undo that but for that to be done we have to use something like alum – the alum of discrimination. One has to put in discrimination and shake the bottle – bring in some discussions based on personal observations, not bookish knowledge. It is only through that one would be able to 'decolourise' oneself and see the pure Self taking charge of all situations.

The colour which we see added to the pure clean Ganges water is the colour of all desires. We are surrounded by our desires and we are producing them every day and covering ourselves with a multitude of desires. One after the other these colours are being added to this pure being, and it is not being seen because of our desires. Because these desires are multiple, they are usually opposed to each other, and a desire which meets opposition raises doubt. So one lives with desires and doubts and because of this it is very difficult to take direct or conscious action. Discrimination, as has been said, is the remedy.

The causal body is known as the inner instrument (*Soul*) which you have heard about. In the *Soul* all the four components are jointed together – synchromeshed; it is a single unit, and there is no division in *Soul* as such. The four parts are for the subtle body where they have to take certain types of action. This unit is the source of temperament out of which come the attitudes underlying different types of desire. These desires first arise in the body mind mechanism, and it is this which arouses the desire. But any desire is always supported by a certain emotional attitude – attitudes of liking or disliking, good or bad. So whenever a given person has a given desire, he takes his attitude to it from the *Soul* which gives it a particular colour, the colour that is in his *Soul*. The moving mind has no particular colour of its own, but it picks it up from the causal body where everything is united.

(taking the *Soul* as an inner organ with four gears synchromeshed or integrated on a higher level –)

The simile is quite suitable. The whole engine and its power would be much like the Almighty together with the *Soul,* from which all the forces are derived that motivate the car. And then the engine can be divided into mechanisms such as the four gears – your sense of 'I', memory, moving mind and discrimination.

In everyone's life one does experience unity with the True Self or Almighty but one does not know it. During deep sleep the Self merges with the Universal Self. This happens in ignorance but is a natural phenomenon. If during active life or meditation one does not feel this merging, it is because of a sheath. This sheath is natural too. The unity which is experienced is the light thrown by the Almighty or True Self on this sheath, and recognised by the *Soul*. If the sheath is transparent and pure, then all is well, but if it is cloudy or dirty, one only gets a glimmer. This is the brink of direct experience. If the water in the Ganges were Universal Self, then water taken from the Ganges and put into a bottle would be the individualised Self, although the water is the same. Once you open or break the bottle letting the water flow back into the Ganges you would no longer see any difference, and you would not be able to take that water back, for it will have merged with the Ganges again and for ever. The only thing which has made it different is the sheath. So the *Soul* separates the individual Self from the Universal Self.

The bridge between the universal and the individual is the *Soul* which is composed of *discrimination, memory and the moving mind.*

Within each individual and within each *Soul* the knowledge of all names and forms with their possibilities are present in a seed form. Unlike the Almighty or True Self, the individual is not aware of these so he doesn't know that he knows. When he grows in his being or is able to clear off his cloud of ignorance then he sees what he has. The need also accounts for such situations as when an individual becomes a medium of inspiration and expression – both.

For the *Soul* there are different limits for different people. For instance, one may become a wrestler and develop his body in strength but there will be a limit to what his constitution would allow. One can refine this causal body according to one's being. When, by disciplined work, the coverings of ignorance are removed one may extend the exercise of power beyond the usual limit. Most of such experiences are possible only for a limited period under certain circumstances.

Frustration comes when one considers only physical help. One can really help very much more on the mental level, but to do that one has to rise high in the subtle world to bring about any workable result. One should meditate more and properly and raise one's level and the necessary help will have gone to the needful even unnoticed. This age seems to have intellectuals and compassionates in abundance but their quality is very coarse. They all wish to help in a violent and agitative way only through the physical means. They do not realise the importance of the subtle world and run amok to do good and so meet with frustrations and produce still more discord. There are very few really peaceful people who would wish to help through the subtle world. Even such men are nowadays surrounded by intellectuals agitating to get them moving. Only one who is desireless, stable and unmoving can get any wisdom and unless one has wisdom one can't help anyone. The potential power of the subtle world is so great that physical world can't begin to use it in its full capacity. When a real impulse is given by such un-moving men, one sees that only a part of it is achieved, but even that is great. Let the intellectuals understand this and do only what is necessary

The four divisions of *Soul* manifest in the subtle body in two places. One centre is felt in the heart, the other in the head. Two of the four components are felt to be stationed in the heart – the temperament or emotional attitude and the memory. The thinking processes, discrimination and the sense of 'I' are stationed in the head. The strength of the heart is greater than the strength of the head. If someone holds something very deadly to his heart – the reason can do little to dislodge this; merely thinking it is right or wrong changes nothing.

The composition of the causal body depends not only on the *Soul*, but the Light of the True Self or Absolute. They are the centre of all conscious power which one feels through the body. But there is a particular place where this is felt first and then it is distributed throughout the body, and this again is how one feels anything which is happening in the body. If you take a mirror you see the image of your face. Ordinary man considers in his ignorance that the image is the real thing. This is one of the illusions – the other factor is the dust or colour which lies on the mirror. Whatever dust or colour is on the mirror will obscure or colour the reflection of the face, which will look ugly or distorted. In fact the face within is never ugly. So the Light of the True Self reflected in the causal level of the *Soul* is pure, and yet because of the contamination of the *Soul* due to fundamental qualities you see things and people in varying colours. The only way to remove the dust and false colour from the mirror is to understand that the image is illusory but the face is real; only the light of pure reason can help to remove both these illusions.

☆

You can see fire as something which emanates heat. Take a ball of iron which is hard and black. When you put both of them together then the iron ball will turn into a red ball of fire. In fact the qualities of both have penetrated each other. In the same way the *Soul* is the materiality into which the light of the True Self, or Consciousness, is put. They both become one. The *Soul* takes the qualities of the Self. This is how this unit functions for the individual and is felt by the individual. The rise of intuitive discrimination is only possible through discoursing with a man of wisdom or those who are wiser than you. Discoursing and trying to get at the truth will bring understanding.

There was a man who had a parrot. This man used to go to visit a wise man, and one day the parrot asked his owner to ask the wise man how it could be liberated. When the owner put this question the wise man said nothing but fell to the ground with his eyes closed. Bystanders rebuked the man for asking so awkward a question as to make the Teacher unconscious, and he was driven away. He returned home and related to the parrot what had happened. The parrot said "That's enough for me". Next morning the parrot copied exactly what the Teacher had done. Its owner found it lying apparently dead on the bottom of the cage so he opened the door. The parrot immediately flew out having found its liberation. So the necessity is there for anyone who seeks liberation to find a true teacher.

Q. You have said that attachment to desires is the cage, and people sometimes ask if that story of the parrot relates to the situation of the True Self. But surely the True Self is perfect?

S. No, the True Self is never bound by anything. But when the *Soul*, which we feel as 'I' is superimposed on the True Self which is the usual state of all of us, even then the Self is just as free as ever. In fact it is not the True Self who is in the cage! The superimposition is caused by attachment, so it would seem that the *Soul* itself gets into the cage because of craving and greed. So there are two possible states for people – first the *Soul* being free from these attachments or secondly *Soul* being in a cage due to them. The Real Self is under no circumstances bound by anything; it is only the *Soul* or psyche. Those who seem to be liberated, or have no cage, experience freedom; those who are not free are bound by their own desires, attachments and greed.

Melting of the heart usually achieves two

things. First of all, because of certain forces coming into play to melt the heart, a cleansing process takes place and all the restlessness or inertia is practically removed from the situation. Once the heart is clear and fluid, then one doesn't have to invite Grace to come into play. Grace comes into play by itself. The cleansing of one's old impressions takes place because of the melting of the heart and something new and different follows which is Grace. This Grace is held firmly because of the abundance of light and purity in the heart. If a glass is clean then the sunlight can come through without any invitation, but the sunlight cannot penetrate if the sides of the glass are opaque and coated with mud. So the Soul has somehow to be cleaned, and this cleansing is possible only through a prayerful attitude and complete submission so that the forces of the Absolute may come into play within the individual and he should then be able to perform his activities under the influence of purity.

Because of three types of coverings which we have communication is hampered and it is not possible to learn from those wiser. One of them is usually predominant in each individual. The first one is opaque dirt which prevents all penetration into the *Soul* of the individual, so that he does not understand anything of what is being presented, or the way being shown to him. The second is distraction which is when wisdom is being passed on but the attention of the individual goes elsewhere just after catching the first sentence, so he cannot listen to what is being said. And the third one is like a sort of veil or covering because of which there is practically no impression gained by the individual. This veil is due to sticking to certain ideas which have been taken without any reason – sort of blind belief. These are the three ways due to which communication of pure reasoning is not possible. One has to get rid of these before reason can prevail. The union or unity of head and heart is essential. When this unity takes place it is the pure *Soul* – the individual is full of purity and light and it is only in this state that something good can prevail. Those who cannot bring their head and heart together, if they are not aligned then distortion takes place and discussion is not understood by them.

The causal body is the combination of the *Soul* and the conscious power of the Divine Self.

Q. As the subtle body can leave the physical body, can the causal body separate from the subtle body, and if so what part is this? Does part of the *Soul* belong to the subtle body and part to the causal body?

S. The separation of the physical body from the other bodies is ordinary knowledge which every one understands, but when it comes to the subtle and causal bodies then it requires true knowledge. Once an individual has acquired true knowledge or knowledge of the Self, then one sees these bodies separated from the Self is illusion, for in fact they are always together because the subtle body is the emanation of the causal body itself.

This spiritual knowledge is like the ocean. A person with a good *Soul* desires to go deeper and deeper. Since there is no end to the depth of this spiritual knowledge the *Soul* cannot take in everything so another and still another effort will have to be made. Those people who think that they have now understood everything and achieved everything in no way understand what knowledge or true happiness really means.

Before one can transform one's nature it is essential to understand what one's nature is. It is the combination of all the four functions which are your ego or sense of 'I', your memory, your moving mind and your discrimination. Your ego gives the feeling of 'I'; your memory holds all the your individual knowledge and cherishes certain thoughts; your discrimination is between what is useful or not useful, and your moving mind is that through which you have desires and counter-desires. If your nature is good and pure, then all these four functions will also be good and pure because your nature is the force which works through these four. When the force is good the instruments function properly. In this way your sense of 'I' will stand for the True Self and not other things like the body or mind but will be universal. Your memory will have good knowledge in store and cherish good ideas. Your discrimination will be pure and will decide what is good for the Self and refuse other considerations, and your moving mind will have good desires only for your development.

Although individuals do feel a separate identity, in reality there is only one identity, and that is the Almighty or Universal Self. In our *Soul* and the subtle body we have this individual being, and because of ignorance and other influences it seems to feel a difference from the Universal Self and that is why it wants to unite with the Universal

Self. For this unity of the individual and the universal it seems as if the effort is being made by the individual himself. The individual, if indeed he does anything at all, only removes the impediments which block his vision of his unity with the Universal Self. In fact, the movement is only from the Universal Self's side. It is the Almighty who reaches out to the individual. Love or devotion should be developed by removing the impediments, and that, of course, is possible through meditation and the attention which one brings into one's life. This, in a way, removes the separate identity of the individual which is composed of his name, his form and his so-called nature. All these things have got to be given up for real unity or for real love towards the Almighty. The effort is, of course, made by the individual, but he makes little effort. The greater effort is made by the Almighty, just as a small being or child has small legs and can only take small steps. The big man can walk quicker and cover more ground. The same applies to the individual who is a very small being, and the Almighty which has no limit. This is how the unity of the individual and the Almighty should be made. All individuals are the Absolute themselves and so are you. It is only a question of realising that one is the Absolute.

Soul is the internal machinery – internal body – and it has got four parts – ego or your sense of 'I', memory, moving mind and discrimination – which are just like four gears in a car, and you use one gear for a particular type of speed. When you use one of these you get a different function.

☆

What is commonly called 'mind' is all contained in the *Soul* or inner organ which on the causal level is all one, but on the subtle level is divided into four different functions. The moving mind is that part which thinks of this and that – "I will do this, I will do that". Your discriminating factor is that which tells you what is right and wrong, and your memory tells you 'Yes, I will do this, I will do that". Your ego says "This is my mind, this is my intellect." It says "my" to everything! So mind is divided into four parts according to different functions that form the basis of knowledge. When we deal with mind we deal with it in accordance with four classifications of its functions.

The first thing to understand is that one should never consider one's shortcomings, one should always take the positive aspect that whatever glory is made available in the form of energy, power, intelligence, wisdom should be put into action. The Universe is designed in such a way that each being has its place and is empowered with certain limited force. Within this limit they will have to do what is most suitable to them. It is true that they can do it better or worse, but always within certain limits So each being is provided with certain assets or talents within his *Soul* which he has to make use of for himself, his family, for his society, in his nation and so on. Each one has to understand how much energy is available to him to use in a particular place and at as particular time. In the Gita, Krishna says the action should be performed with pleasure, not by coercion or compulsion, not by bondage of any sort – so whatever emanates from one's state of being should be performed and then should be forgotten so that the next opportunity may be taken and performed. This relates to the principle that one does not have to think about what one <u>cannot</u> do, one should always keep on thinking about what one <u>can</u> do.

Love and true knowledge are just two names for one and the same thing which is a natural property of the Self and rises spontaneously to the surface when the *Soul* concentrates.

We have to cleanse the *Soul*. There is dirt in it due to the traits of our nature. We remove this dirt by providing light. What is this light? Is it the light of the sun, the moon, electric light or something like that? No, none of these. The light is the light of the Self. We can see the image of the sun in the water, but when there are ripples in the water then the images appear to be quivering. The quivering is in the water, not in the sun! If the water is dirty the image may not be clear, but the dirt exists in the water, not in the sun. What are the methods of purifying and clearing the *Soul*? Good action, holy action, holy thought and service; considering everybody to be part of the same Universal Self; treating other people as our own selves; remembering that the same pure Universal Self permeates all living beings which we come across as a universal brotherhood. These are the things which provide the light to purify our *Soul*. Sun, moon, fire, electricity stand for four of the sources of light. A fifth source is the true knowledge which activates everything. It is not a physical light – vibrations in the ether like the light emitted by the sun, moon etc. but it is a thing which enables us to know. We can call the light of True Knowledge a light but it is unlike the light we get from the sun. It is simply that which enables us to know.

A wise man or teacher is not putting anything into the mind of an ignorant man. There is no transfer of anything – the words of the teacher can only awaken a thing which already existed in the mind of the other person. Here is an example: in the darkness a piece of rope looks like a serpent. Is the serpent in the *Soul* or in the rope? It was in the *Soul* so the removal of the wrong ideas, that is the imparting of knowledge, that is all the words of a Teacher can do.

Difficulty arises because we think our Self is inside us, while the fact is that our *Soul* which includes our mind is within the Self. There is light in this room, but this light is not of the room, it is coming from outside, it is from the sun. So it would be wrong to say the room has light – the source of light is outside the room. So the

Self is outside; the *Soul* is in the Self, not the other way round.

The two active elements of the *Soul* are the moving mind and discrimination. The moving mind is the means of expression for desires to initiate action. This part of the mind is ready to repeat, spontaneously, whatever is pleasant to the senses. Therefore, all that is necessary is for one's discrimination to be made sharper and stronger to control these desires before one acts on impulse. Those who seek true knowledge are usually blessed with reason which can remove all these obstacles.

One needs to be patient and persistent; sooner or later reason will prevail. There may be an element of one's nature which bursts out at unguarded moments to claim it's share of pleasure. Those who are not provided with true knowledge and reason do not know what causes these eruptions. They may even justify them! Men of reason have the capacity to recognise them. This recognition of a failing is itself the proof that discrimination is active. Action done cannot be undone, but men of reason feel sorry to have seen it taking place unintentionally. This sense of remorse creates vigilance and in the light of reason such tendencies lose their strength and in the course of time disappear. There is no obstacle which cannot be removed by reason and wisdom. After all consciousness is not supreme for nothing. Vanity and arrogance are no exceptions. Reason can dissolve them only when one sees the obstacle and feels sorry to have stumbled. There is no external obstacle for obstacles are nothing more than a wrong measure of the goodness provided by the Absolute.

The Sanskrit terminology which has been translated:

Soul:	**Antahkaran(a)**
Discrimination:	**Buddhi**
Memory:	**Chitta**
Moving Mind:	**Manas**
Ego – 'I':	**Ahamkar**
Self:	**Atman**
Universal Self:	**Param -Atman**

The following answer describes these different functions and their role:

"Each one of us lives in three kinds of bodies, viz physical, subtle and causal. The inner organ of mind as a unified whole belongs to the causal body. Functionally this consists of four individual parts on the subtle level: the *moving mind*, 'I' thought, *ego* and *discrimination*, but this inner organ of mind is one and the same thing which, on being activated by the supreme power assumes any one of the four functions and thereby acquires the corresponding name.

The *moving mind* is that which thinks ' I should be having this' or 'I should be having that'. It acts like an office secretary whose job is merely to put up various papers or files before the boss and its duty ends with this. The rest is not its concern and belongs to the realm of other departments of the inner organ of mind.

Memory is that which thinks over what the *moving mind* presents, what would be favourable and what would be unfavourable.

'I' thought is of two kinds, pure and impure. The impure is that which makes us believe ' I am this physical body', 'I am great or small', 'black or white, rich or poor, learned or ignorant' etc. Pure 'I' thought is that which identifies itself with the Real Self or the Universal Self. Everything is only that, and yet it is neither this nor that. For example, the banana is a fruit, but we can call neither its skin, pulp, tree, stem nor leaves a banana and yet a thing called banana is there. Similarly 'I' am neither the hand, feet, head nor even the whole body which is made up of all these. Hence 'I' which is separate from all these if pure 'I'.

Discrimination is that which takes decisions. These decisions govern actions.

The *Universal Self* is in each and everything and yet is neither the whole world or anything it is made up of. But it is all truth, all power, all joy. This is as far as words can go.

The individual *Self* is a part of the *Universal Self*, possessing all the attributes of the *Universal Self* just as water in a drop is a part of the ocean and is endowed with all the properties of the ocean water.

Discrimination

(The division of the *Soul* into four on the subtle or psychological level was a new idea and many questions were asked by the Doctor when he visited India in 1962 and 1964. The key appeared to be the part called one's *Discrimination* or *Intellect* and this appeared to be so important to right living that the following is a selection of the many answers on this subject during these two visits.)

There is a fundamental difference between human beings and non-human beings. Human beings are provided with the faculty of *discrimination* and if they don't use it they can't learn anything; but other kingdoms don't have this faculty. They are guided by their instincts, or one of their senses has super quality. Thus dogs can smell far more acutely than any human being, and with this quality they manage their life. Likewise other species have some extra quality to make their life safe and practical.

Your *Discrimination* is like your machine (tape recorder.) If you tune it towards purity it will give purity. If you tune it the other way – towards passion or inertia, you cannot get purity. In the life of a disciple the chief problem is to make his *discrimination* clean and precise so that he will be able to distinguish what is, from what is not.

Q. Is an example of it being tuned in the wrong direction the strife between religious sects and the persecution of heretics – all that?

S. Wars in the name of religion and sectarian differences are the product of confusion in the faculty of *Discrimination*. When the latter is not related to the True Self these things manifest in the activities of these people.

Q. Would you tell us the chief way to make our *Discrimination* pure?

S. Love the Truth and leave the untruth. That is the cure.

Pursuit of *Truth* cures and clears the *Discrimination;* just in this single activity both are achieved; the Truth comes and the *Discrimination* is cleared and cleaned. But if the direction is the other way, with the pursuit of the untruth, then the *Discrimination* becomes muddled and the result is pain and suffering.

Discrimination is subordinate to the Self, and whatever it does, it does at the bidding of the Self. When it is turned towards this world then it gets lost and it forgets. It forgets that the source is the Self. And that is why it gets disturbed, perturbed and loses tranquillity. But when it is turned towards God Almighty, towards the Self, then it remembers its source and then it becomes steady and attains liberation.

As we are our *Discrimination* is not clear – it is so fast, busy and entangled that it cannot properly exert its influence. We are always full of desires and doubts – both. *Discrimination* is provided but it can discriminate only if it is still. The light of the Self reflects through the *Discrimination* but if it is in movement it is unable to reflect. One needs to still it, give rest. A machine much used gets hot and needs rest to cool down. So does the *Discrimination*. After a good deep sleep one finds oneself fresh, and also after meditation one comes out with clear *Discrimination*.

Discrimination in pure state works like a mother. She cares and works for the betterment of the child and protects from dangers and difficulties, warns of impending dangers and keeps it away from bad influences. *Discrimination* in pure state reminds one and chases one to work for betterment. Good company enhances the chances of development and bad company would dim it out.

Discrimination is like a manager or chief minister of state.. If it is pure then the management will be efficient and the state will be run in such a way that the true

King rules over it for the happiness and prosperity of the subjects. If the *Discrimination* is corrupt, then every section of the state would be corrupt and unruly. This would result in misery of the subjects and captivity of the King. Our body is also like a state with a King (the Self) and hundreds of servants and subjects to please him. Weak or corrupt *Discrimination* will wreck the whole system and ruin the Self. A pure *Discrimination* will command the whole system to get the best for the subjects and proper due to the King.

If you take a stick, light it at one end and rotate it vigorously, then you will see multifarious shapes of light but not the stick or the fire at the end. Such is the mobile *Discrimination*. This must be stilled. True Knowledge removes the dirt or cloud and meditation stills it. By such discipline one purifies the *Discrimination* so it will show the right path.

A cloud surrounds our *Discrimination* and ignorance is the cause. Although *Discrimination* receives light from the Self, when it presumes that the light is its own and concludes that everything it has observed is right, then it is impure; when it understands it derives light from the Self and claims nothing for itself, then it is pure. Its mobility or speed is one of the great stumbling blocks in seeing the Truth.

Notes:

*Dom Bede Griffiths 1906 – 1993 of the Christian Ashram, "Shantivanam", in Tamil Nadu, South India. and author of many books.

** Dr. Francis Roles, 1901 -1982, founder of The Study Society.

***His Holiness Shantanand Saraswati, Shankaracharya of Jyotirmath whom Dr. Roles first met in 1961. Dr. Roles visited him at the Ashram in Allahabad, and once in Lucknow. Following the death of Dr. Roles, Maureen Allan and representatives of the Study Society continued to visit the Shankaracharya on behalf of the Society at the Ashram in Allahabad until his retirement when they saw him at other venues there and latterly in New Delhi, the last visit being made in 1993. His Holiness died in 1997. He never sought a personal following in the West and would only see Dr. Roles or one or two representatives of the Society, saying that this knowledge is universal and should be manifested in each person's own country and religious tradition. For everyone he advocated meditation, and all his meetings began with a period of silent meditation.